Copper Canyon Press
Port Townsend

THE
SILVER
SWAN

poems written in Kyoto 1974-75

Kenneth Rexroth

Special Thanks to: *Patti Pattee and Bill O'Daly; Jo Cochran; Centrum Foundation, Fort Worden State Park, where Copper Canyon is press-in-residence; & the National Endowment for the Arts, a federal agency.*

Copper Canyon Press
Box 271
Port Townsend, WA 98368

THE
SILVER
SWAN

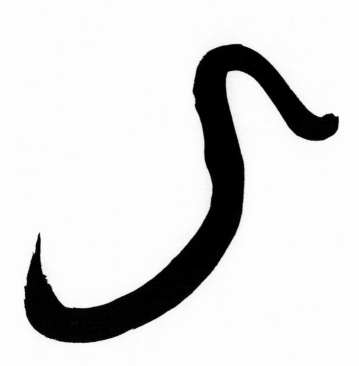

For Ruth Stephan

Twilit snow,
The last time I saw it
Was with you.
Now you are dead
By your own hand
After great pain.
Twilit snow.

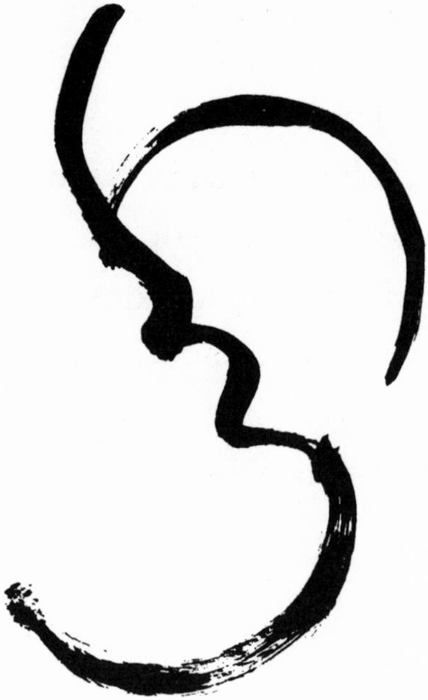

As the full moon rises
The swan sings
In sleep
On the lake of the mind.

Orange and silver
Twilight over Yoshino.
Then the frosty stars,
Moving like crystals against
The wind from Siberia.

Under the half moon
The field crickets are silent.
Only the cricket
Of the hearth still sings, louder
Still, behind the gas heater.

Late night, under the
Low, waning eleventh month
Moon, wild frosted kaki
On the bare branches gleam like
Pearls. Tomorrow they
Will be sweet as the
Honey of summer.

Asagumori

On the forest path
The leaves fall. In the withered
Grass the crickets sing
Their last songs. Through dew and dusk
I walk the paths you once walked,
My sleeves wet with memory.

Void Only

I cannot escape from you.
When I think I am alone,
I awake to discover
I am lost in the jungle
Of your love, in its darkness
Jewelled with the eyes of unknown
Beasts. I awake to discover
I am a forest ascetic
In the impenetrable
Void only, the single thought
Of which nothing can be said.

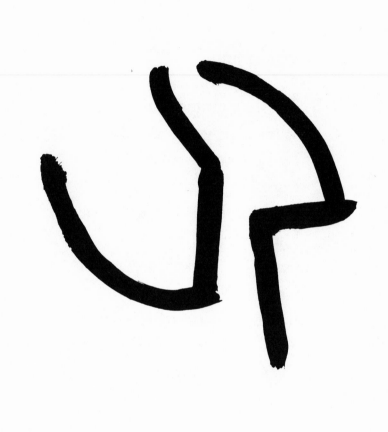

Seven Seven

Can I come to you
When the cowboy comes to the
Weaving girl? No sea is as
Wide as the River of Heaven.

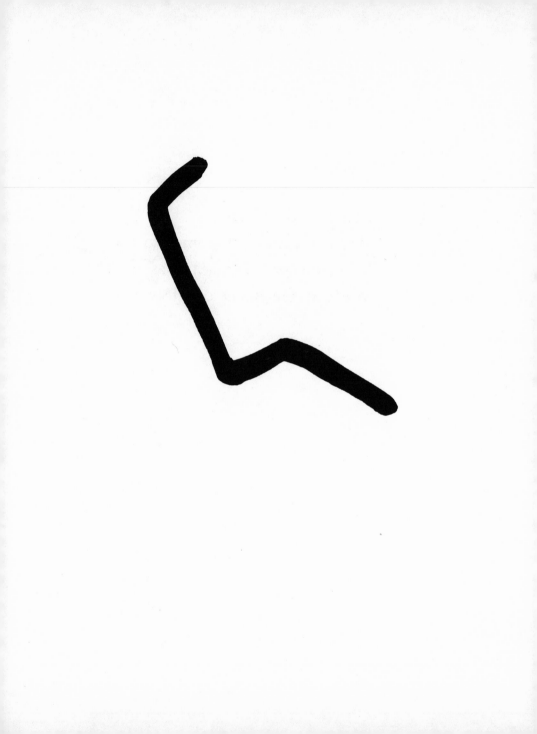

The new moon has reached
The half. It is utterly
Incredible. One
Month ago we were strangers.

After Akiko—*"Yoru no cho ni"*

For Yasuyo

In your frost white kimono
Embroidered with bare branches
I walk you home New Year's Eve.
As we pass a street lamp
A few tiny bright feathers
Float in the air. Stars form on
Your wind blown hair and you cry,
"The first snow!"

Late Spring.
Before he goes, the uguisu
Says over and over again
The simple lesson no man
Knows, because
No man can ever learn.

Bride and groom,
The moon shines
Above the typhoon.

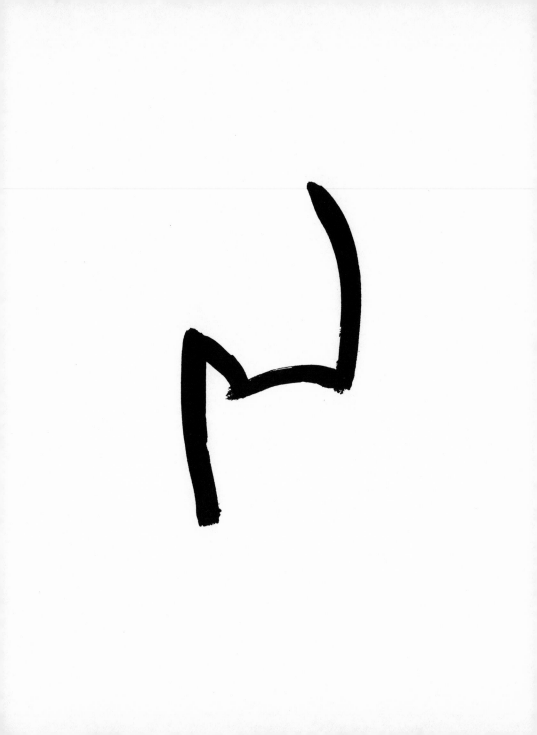

Only the sea mist,
Void only.
Only the rising
Full moon,
Void only.

Hototogisu—horobirete

The cuckoo's call, though
Sweet in itself, is hard to
Bear, for it cries,
"Perishing! Perishing!"
Against the Spring.

Tsukutsukuboshi

In the month of great heat
The first bell cricket cries.
"It is time to leave."

New Year

The full moon shines on
The first plum blossoms and opens
The Year of the Dragon.
May happy Dragons
Attend you with gifts of joy.

100 copies printed on Rives buff paper in 18 pt. Centaur type September 1976 by Sam Hamill and Tree Swenson, Copper Canyon Press, and bound in cloth over boards by Lincoln & Allen, Portland.

2000 copies photo-offset from the letterpress proofs and bound in wrappers.

The brushwork is by Carol Tinker.